HOW TO DEVELOP AN INNOVATION TALENT SUCCESSION PLAN

Tools for Creating Innovation Skills Bench-Strength in Organizations

HOW TO DEVELOP AN INNOVATION TALENT SUCCESSION PLAN

Tools for Creating Innovation Skills Bench-Strength in Organizations

DAVID MASUMBA

Printed in the United States of America

ISBN Paperback: 978-1-7341913-5-6

ISBN eBook: 978-1-7341913-9-4

To my beloved family, Mujina, Waana and Luwi

CONTENTS

PREFACE

For more than ten years, I've been engaged in workforce innovation. I've interacted with many organizational leaders on the topic of workforce innovation. I've conducted reviews of many studies and publications on the topic of workforce innovation. My experience is that while most organizational leaders acknowledge that understanding the current and future innovation talent needs of the organization is critical in creating and sustaining an innovation-led organization, many organizations do not seem to have the necessary tools for creating a mechanism to monitor their current and future innovation talent. In other words, most organizations need to create an organizational framework that ensures that the organization has workforces with a mixture of innovation skill sets to meet the current and future innovation performance needs.

This is where this book comes in. This book prescribes how to create an innovation talent succession plan. It provides tools for creating a pool of workforces with the right mix of innovation skill sets so that the innovation performance of functional units and the achievement of short or long-term innovation goals are not negatively affected in case of innovation talent departures.

Chapter 1

INTRODUCTION

Chapter one focuses on the following three aspects:

1. Reason for this book
2. Definition of innovation talent succession planning
3. Objectives of the book
4. Structure of the book

Below are details of each of the above aspects.

1. Reasons for this Book

This book is based on the following four premises:

Organizations are now seeking to broaden innovation capabilities across functional units

According to studies on innovation, many organizations have realized that the traditional approach of relying on specific functional units and few individuals for innovation exposes an organization to the risk of not matching up to the organization's demands for innovation.

In a study by Deloitte on *Human Capital Trends*, it was observed that today's innovation leaders are now defining innovation broadly to include a wide range of issues across the enterprise. Other studies have echoed similar sentiments. The new notion is that many organizations are making every employee be involved in driving innovation. This approach means that organizations must build capability for ensuring a sustainable supply chain of innovative ideas across all functional units. One such capability is having a mechanism that ensures that organizations have effective tools for determining the following:

- Current innovation performance needs
- Current innovation skill set needs
- Future innovation performance needs
- Future innovation skill set needs

Innovation talent succession planning is one of the vital tools to determine and address the above issues.

It's too risky to rely on just a few workforces to drive innovation

As stated earlier, the conventional approach to innovation in organizations has been that innovation is the responsibility of specific functional units and professionals. Relying on few functional units and individuals to power and sustain the organization's innovation pipeline exposes organizations to the vulnerabilities of the effects of the departure of innovation talent on innovation performance at the organization.

For example, according to a Forbes online publication, Apple lost about 150 of their innovation talent and executives to Tesla between 2008 and 2015. This book contests that in order to mitigate the effect of losing innovation talent on the innovation performance of functional units, organizations should adopt effective innovation talent succession mechanisms.

The intention of this book is to arm organizational leaders with tools that ensure that the innovation pipeline of the organization is not negatively affected when innovative talents depart or when innovation performance slumps because the organization didn't have strong innovation-talent bench strength.

Concerns about workforce movements

According to a number of analysts, one of the major concerns of executives in highly innovative companies regarding workforce changes includes:

- Prospects of losing their highly innovative staff
- Difficulties in finding new workers with high innovative potential
- Difficulties in finding innovation talent with the right mix of innovation skills
- Lack of bench-strength to replace highly innovative individuals when they depart

The above concerns or issues would be mitigated by adopting innovation talent succession mechanisms. On the other hand, the situation would even be worse if the organization has not adopted innovation talent succession programs.

Escalating skill shortages

A number of talent-related surveys suggest that many companies across the globe are facing challenges in finding the right talent. For instance, according to the Chartered Institute of Professional Development (CIPD)/ Hays survey titled *Resourcing and Talent Planning Survey in the UK*, skill shortages are escalating. The survey report was based on responses from 520 organizations, and over 80 percent felt that competition for talent has increased over the past two years. Similarly, surveys conducted by ManpowerGroup, a U.S. based human resources consulting company, revealed a steady rise in the number of companies experiencing difficulties in finding job candidates with the right skills. In a survey by KPMG, the majority of respondents—about 59 percent—agreed that there is a new war for talent and that the skill shortages are likely to increase. How do these skill shortages across industries relate to innovation talent?

In today's innovation-driven global economy, for a company to compete it has to attract and hire diverse innovation talent to meet short-term and long-term needs. However, finding job candidates with right innovation skills is even more difficult, especially since innovation is now the top priority in most companies. For instance, in Boston Consulting Group's survey of the 2015 Most Innovative Companies, 80 percent of respondents indicated innovation as being either a top priority or top three priority at their company. Yet, many companies find it hard to hire job candidates with the right innovation skill sets to drive their innovation agenda. In a 2017 PWC survey, 77 percent of CEOs struggle to find the innovation skills they need.

With that being said, it is absolutely necessary for organizations that desire to create a culture of innovation to implement strategies that ensure that the organization has, at any given time, a sufficient mix of innovation talent needed to achieve short and long term innovation goals and to sustain an innovation-driven organization.

Definition

In order to understand what innovation talent succession planning entails, it is important to understand the meaning of succession planning. Generally, succession planning is defined as the process where an organization ensures that employees are hired, developed, and prepared to fill roles left vacant due to resignation, termination, transfer, promotion, retirement, or death. The process involves developing and preparing employees with specific knowledge, skills, and abilities for future functional roles in the organization.

That being said, we define innovation talent succession planning as: *a framework of tools for creating a pool of workforces with right mix of innovation skill sets so that achievement of short or long term innovation goals is not affected in functional units in case of innovation talent departures due to resignation, termination, transfer, promotion, retirement, or death.*

In other words, innovation talent succession planning ensures that the organization has sufficient "innovation skills bench-strength".

Meaning of innovation skills bench-strength?

From a conventional human resource planning perspective, "*bench-strength*" is a figurative term used to describe the competence levels and number of employees ready to fill a vacancy if a substantive position holder left.

In the context of innovation talent succession planning, "innovation skills bench- strength"; is a process that involves determining the preparedness of an organization in terms of having the right number of staff with adequate levels of innovation skills to fill the gaps in case the organization experiences some innovation talent departures, thereby, ensuring that the innovation performance capability of an organization is not adversely affected when such departures occur.

2. Structure of the Book

This book is structured in 15 steps for designing and implementing *innovation talent succession planning*. The book is divided in five chapters.

Chapter 2

PREREQUISITES

There are six steps in this chapter:

- Step 1: Assessing Current Situation
- Step 2: Describing the Organizational Vision
- Step 3: Outlining the Core and Support Functional Units
- Step 4: Understanding the Meaning of Innovation
- Step 5: Understanding Innovation Dimensions
- Step 6: Aligning the Meaning of Innovation to Functional Units and Business Segments

Step 1: Assessing Current Situation

Assessing current situation is the first step for creating and implementing an innovation talent succession mechanism. The process involves determining whether the organization has included some elements of innovation talent succession planning in the organization`s existing overall HR succession planning practice.

To understand the *current situation* in the context of innovation talent succession planning, the first step includes: (1) the definition of assessing current situation in the context of innovation talent succession planning (2) why it's important to assess current situation, (3) an example of a simple table for assessing current situation, and (4) the context of innovation talent succession planning, and (5) CEO must support the exercise.

Definition of *Assessing Current Situation*

We define assessing current situation in the context of innovation talent succession planning as follows: *as a process that involves assessing an organization's existing human resources planning process to determine the extent to which innovation talent succession planning is included.*

Importance

Assessing current situation provides data that informs the leadership of what aspects should be included in the innovation talent succession planning framework and to what extent certain innovation talent succession planning tools and techniques should be adopted.

Example

Here is an example of a table for assessing current situation when creating the innovation talent succession planning mechanism.

Table 2:1. Example of a Table for Assessing Current Situation

Assessing Current Talent Succession Planning Practices	
Elements of the organization's talent succession planning practices: *What are the main aspects of the organization's talent succession planning practices*?	**Has the organization included some aspects of innovation talent succession in the existing human resources planning practices?** If so, outline how:
Conducted by:	
Date assessment was conducted:	

CEO Must Support the Exercise

For any major innovation-support initiative to succeed, CEO support is critical. Adopting an innovation talent succession planning framework is a major innovation-support undertaking that requires unwavering support of the CEO and top leadership of the organization. So, ensure that the idea of introducing an innovation talent recruitment framework is well supported by the top leadership, including the CEO, because without gaining sufficient mindshare and support of the CEO, it will be a huge uphill exercise that will result in a flop.

Many studies have observed that it's almost impossible to systemize innovation across the organization and make it part of the organizational culture without the support of the CEO. When asked in an interview with the *Harvard Business Review Publishing* about the role of CEO in advancing and sustaining innovation across the organization, former Chairman and CEO for Procter & Gamble A.G. Lafley responded that no innovation thrives in an organization without support of the CEO. Lafley is credited for his "*leadership for innovation strategy*" which he initiated since taking over as President and CEO of P&G in 2002 and created a collaborative culture in which innovation was every employee's job. In a survey of 601 senior executives by Accenture on "*Overcoming Barriers to Innovation*", one of the key findings was that the role of the CEO in driving innovation performance in an organization was critical.

In short, the role and support of the top leadership in the organization, beginning with the CEO in advancing and sustaining the culture of innovation across the organization is a key requirement. And since adopting an innovation talent succession planning is one of the key aspects of systemizing innovation across functional units, CEO support is vital.

The bottom line is that the CEO should, directly or indirectly, be involved in establishing various committees that will be responsible for overseeing the process of designing and implementing an organization-wide innovation talent succession planning mechanism.

Step 2: Describe the Organizational Vision

This section involves describing pertinent aspects of the organizational vision and how they relate to innovation talent succession planning activities. The aspects include: (1) definition of organizational vision, (2) why it's important to understand the relationship between organizational vision and innovation talent succession planning, and (3) perspectives of organizational vision.

Definition

What is an organizational vision? Organizations use different phrases to define their organizational vision. A company vision is a picture expressed in the form of a statement, of what the organization would like to be in a defined time period. The latter part of the definition is what distinguishes a *vision* from a *strategy*—an aspect that is often misunderstood by many organizations.

An organizational vision is normally what the organization would like to be in the next three to five years, for instance. The strategy is how the company is going to realize that vision.

In many cases, companies have different perspectives on how to formulate their visions. Some companies have a one-sentence vision statement; others take a multi-dimensional approach in which the organizational vision is expressed from more than one perspective, such as two, three, or four perspectives focusing on core concepts. For example, one company's organizational vision might consist of the following four vision perspectives:

- *Market share vision perspective*—which takes into account what the company intends to be like in relation to market share within a defined timeframe.
- *Market leadership vision perspective*—which outlines the company's vision to be a market leader over a specified timeframe.
- *Revenue vision perspective*—outlines the financial vision of the company over a specified period. In other words, how much revenue does the company intend to generate in the next three to five years?

- *Shareholder value vision perspective*—which outlines the desired percentage of growth in dividends over a specified period.

The bottom line is that whatever style or approach the organization adopts to formulate the organizational vision, it must be simple, clear, and be understood by everyone in the organization.

Importance

Why is it important to understand the relationship between organizational vision and innovation talent succession planning? The essence of the innovation talent succession planning is to ensure that the organization always has the right number of workforces and type of innovation skill sets to achieve both functional unit and corporate innovation goals, ultimately contributing toward realizing the overall vision of the organization. In other words, in order to achieve functional unit and corporate innovation goals, in which realization of the organizational vision depends, the organization needs to have the right numbers of workforces and type of innovation skill sets in case of innovation talent departures; then the innovation performance of the organization is not adversely affected.

Step 3: Outlining the Core and Support Functional Units

What does outlining core and support functional units entail? Normally, an organization is configured in structures, depending on its type of business model and vision. However, in whatever way it is structured, there are two structural categories that every organization consists of: core and support (back-office) functional units. This section describes core and support functions in relation to innovation talent succession plan. This includes: (1) interpretation of core and support functional units, (2) the importance of outlining core and support functional units, and (3) the illustration of core and support functional units.

Interpreting Core and Support Functional Units

Core functional units are centered on the organization's main or essential business activities. Usually, core functional units are those that are directly involved in driving the organization's mission. For instance, in a furniture manufacturing company, the design and production functional units would be considered "core", whereas, finance and accounting units would be support functional units. Also, core units vary from organization to organization, depending on the business model and size.

Support functional units comprise functional activities that are aimed at supporting achievement of strategic goals and targets of the organization's core business activities. Further, characteristics of functional units vary from organization to organization, depending on the business model and size.

Importance

Why is it important to outline core and support functional units? Innovation talent succession planning does not occur in a vacuum, but in job positions of functional roles. That being said, it is necessary to review of all the functional activities in both core and support function units and all positions, determine how the organization's mission-critical job positions are structured, then figure out how to imbed a mechanism for innovation talent succession across the organization. In other words, you cannot implement innovation talent succession planning process effectively without understanding how the functional unit roles and job positions of the organization are structured.

Illustration of Core and Support Functional Units

Let's take the example of Nada Bank, a fictitious company. Assuming Nada Bank provides many banking services. There are two activities to be conducted:

First, identify core and support functional units of Nada Bank. Let's assume the bank has the following functional units:

Core units

- Corporate banking department
- Retail banking department

- E-payments department
- Channel banking department
- Money transfer department
- Marketing department
- Customer service department

Support unit

- HR department
- Finance & accounting department
- IT department
- Corporate affairs department

Second, review all functional roles in each job position across all functional units.

Step 4: Understanding the Meaning of Innovation

Lack of understanding the meaning of innovation can be a hindrance to effective implementation and adoption of the innovation talent succession planning. In other words, it's not possible to undertake the process of innovation talent succession planning if to start with one has little understanding of the meaning of innovation.

That being said, this section includes: (1) the importance of understanding the meaning of innovation in relation to innovation talent succession planning process, (2) the definition of innovation, and (4) the characteristics of innovative ideas.

Importance

The reason why it is important to understand the meaning of innovation in relation to innovation talent succession planning is that the ultimate aim of the innovation talent succession planning is to ensure that an organization has a pool of sufficient talent with right mix of innovation skill sets to meet the current and future innovation performance needs of the organization. However, a clear understanding of the current and future needs of the organization would only be possible if, to start with, the leadership and the workforces understand the meaning of innovation in the context of the organization's business model and functional activities or units.

In other words, an innovation talent succession planning exercise is exclusively about identifying and building innovation skill sets to meet the current and future innovation needs of the organization. Without having a good grasp of the meaning of innovation, it is impossible to understand innovation skills and innovation performance duties, let alone be able to design and enact an effective innovation talent succession planning process.

Definition

This book defines innovation as a four-part process that involves the following:

Figure 2:1. Definition of Innovation

i) Identifying a problem or need (e.g. within a particular customer/ market segment or your organizational system)	ii) Generating innovative ideas never seen on the market before to fix the identified problem/need
iii) Transforming the innovative ideas (through an established process) into a solution not seen on the market before	iv) Converting the innovative solution into monetary value (i.e. in terms of increased revenue or cost reduction)

Characteristics of Innovative Ideas

Having described the meaning of innovation, we now look at the characteristics of innovative ideas. Understanding characteristics of innovative ideas is vital and necessary for both the leadership and the workforces because, for the most part, workforces will be evaluated on their innovative ideas. So, based on the definition of innovation, the characteristics of an innovative idea are:

- New and offering benefits not seen on the market before
- Aims at meeting customer needs or solving customer problems in a superior manner than before
- Contributes monetary value to the organization

Step 5: Understanding Dimensions of Innovation

We have so far discussed the meaning of innovation and the characteristics of innovative ideas, as well as why it is important to understand these terminologies when it comes to implement and applying innovation talent succession planning process. Step five looks at the concept of *dimensions of innovation* and how that relates to the concept of hiring for innovation. To do this, we need to consider the following: (1) the definition of dimensions of innovation and (2) why it is important to understand dimensions of innovation in relation to innovation talent succession planning.

Definition

The term 'dimensions of innovation' means that innovation occurs in different contexts of organizational activities; dimensions of innovation describe the different ways in which innovation occurs (i.e., *where*) and the degree of change or newness that innovation entails (i.e., *how*).

In a nutshell, 'dimensions of innovation' is a term that describes two related innovation concepts: *types of innovation* and *innovation degree*.

Types of Innovation

Remember, dimension of innovation is a concept used to describe two aspects of innovation: *where* and *how* innovation occurs. Types of innovation relates to the context (*where*) in which innovation occurs in the organization's value chain or functional activities. That said, it is vital to understand that innovation occurs in a variety of functional activities across the organization's value chain. For instance, there are innovation ideas (or innovations) in different contexts of products depending on the nature of an organization's product platforms. There are also process innovation ideas, depending on the nature of an organization, marketing innovations, customer service innovations, and a whole host of service innovations. Further details about types of innovation are covered in Chapter Eight of my book, *Leadership for Innovation.*

Innovation Degree

As stated earlier, dimension of innovation is a concept used to describe two aspects of innovation: *where* it occurs and *how* it occurs. We have so far talked about types of innovation which entails *where* it occurs.

This section looks at *how* innovation occurs in any form or type of innovation, which is referred to as innovation degree—one of the two aspects or concepts of the dimensionality of innovation. This concept is based on the perception that innovative ideas create or add value in varying degrees or extents. Therefore, innovation degree can be defined as the perception of the extent of the newness or novelty of an innovative idea.

Further details on innovation degree are also covered in chapter eight of *Leadership for Innovation.*

Importance

Why is it important to understand dimensions of innovation in relation to innovation talent succession planning? Three reasons:

Innovative ideas are generated in the context of dimensions of innovation

Innovation talent or innovation performance does not occur in a vacuum. Usually, workforces express their innovation talent or innovation performance (as we shall see later) through generation of innovative ideas in the context of various dimensions of innovation of the organization's business model or functional units, such as generation of radical or incremental product, process, marketing, etc.

The leadership is able to understand the innovation capabilities of the organization

By understanding what dimensions of innovation entail in the context of the organization's business model and functional units, organizational leaders are able to determine and understand a number of vital aspects pertaining to the organization's innovation performance capabilities, such as supply chain of innovation ideas across functional units, how diverse the organization's capabilities are, areas of innovation priority, and areas of innovation strength and weaknesses, using the data to inform in the process of designing and implementing innovation talent succession planning, thereby contributing to making the organization's mission of being innovation-led a reality and sustainable.

Helps to understand and create diversity of innovation talent

Having an organization that generates diverse innovation ideas is a critical capability to creating and sustaining an innovation-led organization. However, an organization can only build the capability of diversity of innovative ideas if there is a pool of workforces with an adequate mix of innovation skills to generate innovative ideas of types and varying degree across functional units. The process of creating a mix of innovation talent that can generate diverse innovative ideas across functional units requires one to understand what dimensionality of innovation ideas entails in the context of the organization's business model and functional units.

Step 6: Interpret Meaning of Innovation in the Context of Functional Units

When defining innovation in step four, we stated that it is impossible to understand innovation skills and innovation performance duties, let alone be able to design and enact an effective innovation talent succession planning process without understanding the meaning of innovation. This section is a continuation of Step Four. Step Six looks at the interpretation of the meaning of innovation in the context of the organization's business model and functional units. This section covers the importance of interpreting the meaning of innovation in the context of the organization's business model and functional units in relation to creating a mechanism for innovation talent succession planning.

Importance

Why is it important to interpret the meaning of innovation in the context of the organization's business model or functional units in relation to innovation talent succession planning? Three reasons:

Easy to build innovation talent pool that accurately mirrors innovation needs of the organization

The introduction of this book stated that studies have revealed that innovation is a top priority in many organizations. In other words, many organizations are seeking to be innovation-led organizations. However, for an organization to be truly innovation-led, it means that the leadership must drive innovation performance across functional units. Driving innovation performance across functional units of the organization requires creating a pool of sufficient talent with right mix of innovation skill sets to meet current and future innovation performance needs of the organization.

How is this relevant to interpreting the meaning of innovation in the context of functional units and innovation talent succession planning? It is only when you understand the meaning of innovation in the context of the organization's business model and functional units can it be easy to build an innovation talent pool that accurately mirrors and aligns with the current and future specific innovation talent needs of the organization. In other words, if innovation is not defined in the context of the business model and functional units, it would render the organization's innovation talent succession planning process hard to undertake, because, by its nature, innovation talent is usually contextual. In that, an organization would comprise workforces with different innovation skills that are related to their functional roles, such as product development or marketing. The context of innovation skills would only be clear and easy to understand by workforces if innovation is defined in the context of their roles or functional units. This would make it easier to implement the innovation talent succession planning across the organization.

Makes it easy to understand innovation management-related issues

Interpreting the meaning of innovation in the context of the organization's business model and functional units makes it easy to understand various aspects of innovation management-related issues across functional units such as innovation goals, innovation strategies and, innovation roles of various job positions. These aspects play a vital role and are part of the process of identifying and determining innovation skill gaps, and building innovation skills bench-strength, which are the fulcrum of the innovation talent succession planning process. In Chapter One, we defined innovation skills bench-strength as a process that involves determining the preparedness of an organization in terms of having the right number of staff with adequate levels of innovation skills to fill the gaps in case the organization experiences some innovation talent departures.

Helps the process of creating a diverse pool of innovation talent

Many people in organizations have misconceptions about the meaning of innovation and what it entails. To many, it means generating innovative ideas in certain areas only, such as products or technological-related things. A narrow understanding of innovation can hinder the organization's efforts of developing a broader and diverse pool of innovation talent across functional units. On the other hand, the interpretation of the meaning of innovation in context of the business model and functional units helps in developing and creating a diverse pool of innovation talent to meet the organization's current and future innovation performance needs, which is the fulcrum and essence of innovation talent succession planning.

Details on how to interpret the meaning of innovation in the context of the organization's business model and functional units are also covered in chapter eight (subtitled *Institutionalizing and Educating Workforces about the Meaning of Innovation*) of *Leadership for Innovation.*

Chapter 3

FUNDAMENTAL ELEMENTS

Recall, the introduction to this book states that it's structured in 15 steps detailing how to create a framework for designing and implementing innovation talent succession planning. Chapter Two covered the first six steps. Chapter Three looks at four steps:

- Step 7: Understanding Factors Driving Innovation
- Step 8: Creating Worksheets for Outlining Position Title, Job descriptions and Job Specifications
- Step 9: Interpreting Innovation Skills
- Step 10: Creating Innovation Performance Goals in Core and Support Functional Units

Details of the above aspects are as follows:

Step 7: Understanding Factors Driving Innovation in the Organization

Usually, organizations adopt innovation strategies and performance approaches in response to various internal and external factors. As part of the process for creating a mechanism for innovation talent succession, one of the preliminary aspects to undertake is it to review and relate internal and external factors influencing or driving the need for the organization to adopt a mechanism for innovation talent succession.

That being said, Step Seven includes: (1) the definition of internal and external factors, (2) why it's important to understand how internal and external factors relate to innovation talent succession, and (3) an example of a simple worksheet that can be applied to describe internal and external factors, and how the factors can be aligned to innovation talent succession planning process.

Definition

Internal and external factors are factors obtainable in the business environment that, in one way or another, affect the organization's existence, activities, and future direction, therefore, influence the need for the organization to sustain innovation performance.

Importance

Why is it important to understand internal and external factors influencing innovation when undertaking innovation talent succession planning across functional units?

As stated before, innovation talent succession planning is implemented in specific job positions in the context of the functional roles of each functional unit of the organization. How does this relate to understanding internal and external factors? In that, when taking stock of innovation skill sets across functional units, you do so in relation to current and future innovation performance needs of the organization. In most cases, the current and future innovation performance needs emanate from internal and external factors that the leadership have identified and prioritized. Some of the internal factors that influence innovation strategy of the organization include growth through innovation in non-traditional areas, implementation of cost-saving innovation strategies, or investment in innovation research to develop new products over a specified period. Based on the internal factors identified, the leadership will use the data to help determine about the mix of innovation talent needed for the whole process of innovation talent succession across functional units. Examples of external drivers of innovation include increased competition, emerging growth prospects in certain spaces of business, government regulation, and economic downturns. The context of each of the internal and external factors cited here is described in detail in Chapter Eight (subtitled *Educating Workforces About the Drivers of Innovation*) of *Leadership for Innovation.*

Example

The table below is an example of how internal and external factors can be applied in functional units when conducting innovation talent succession planning.

Table 2-1. Application of Internal and external factors

<table>
<tr><td colspan="4">Name of Department:</td></tr>
<tr><td colspan="4">Category of the Department (core or support functional unit):</td></tr>
<tr><td colspan="4">Position:</td></tr>
<tr><td colspan="4">Date on which assessment of factors is being conducted:</td></tr>
<tr><td>Internal and external factors driving innovation in the functional unit</td><td colspan="3">In light of the internal and external factors stated in the table, outline the category of innovation skill sets which would need a high number of staff with such skills</td></tr>
<tr><td rowspan="2"></td><td>Innovative thinking skills</td><td>Innovation engagement skills</td><td>Innovation management skills</td></tr>
<tr><td></td><td></td><td></td></tr>
<tr><td colspan="4">Names and position of staff conducting assessment:</td></tr>
</table>

Step 8: Review and Collect Data from Job Positions and Innovation Functional Roles

Remember, the purpose of the innovation talent succession mechanism is to enable the organization to have an adequate mix of innovation talent to meet current and future innovation needs of the organization. It is important to know that achieving this requires accurate data collection from job positions and functional roles across the organization. It is therefore necessary to include an activity that involves the review and collection of essential data from job positions and functional roles. That being said, step eight includes: (1) why it's important to review and collect data from job positions and innovation functional roles and (2) reviewing current innovation functional roles and innovation skills in each functional unit.

Importance

Why is it important to review and collect data in job positions and innovation functional roles when conducting the innovation talent succession planning?

As stated on a number of times, the main purpose of innovation talent succession planning is to have adequate innovation talent to meet current and future innovation goals and needs of functional units based on the organization's vision and corporate innovation strategy. In other words, innovation talent succession planning serves the purpose of ensuring that the organization's innovation performance is not adversely affected when staff with particular innovation skill sets leave a job position. How does this relate to reviewing and collection of innovation roles and innovation skills-related data? In Chapter One, we talked about creating the "innovation skills bench-strength", which was defined as "a process that involves determining the preparedness of an organization in terms of having the right number of staff with adequate levels of innovation skills to fill the gaps in case the organization experiences some innovation talent departures". You can only build adequate or required "innovation skills bench-strength" in terms of meeting current and future demands of innovation performance duties of various positions if data regarding position titles, functional roles/job descriptions, and job specifications are accurately gleaned and is fit for purpose. Hence, the importance of reviewing and collecting data about current innovation functional roles and innovation skill sets from job positions across functional units.

Reviewing Current Innovation Functional Roles and Innovation Skills

There are a number of activities and steps to be undertaken when reviewing and creating innovation roles or innovation performance job descriptions and job specifications in functional units. Chapter Eleven of the *Leadership for Innovation* describes how to create innovation-performance job descriptions and job specifications.

Step 9: Understanding Innovation-Challenge Questions

Chapter One and Two defined innovation as: a process that involves identifying a problem, then generating an innovative idea—never seen on the market before to fix the problem—and transforming the innovative idea into a solution, then converting the innovative solution into monetary value. The definition of innovation is in part linked to the old saying: "Necessity is the mother of invention". This saying simply means that situations or challenges inspire the generation of novel solutions at different levels of society: organizations, communities and individuals. In organizations, there are different ways of inspiring innovative ideas or solutions.

One of the effective techniques for inspiring or influencing innovative ideas from workforces is by formulating innovation-challenge questions. That being said, this section includes: (1) the definition of innovation-challenge questions and (2) the importance of innovation-challenge questions in relation to innovation talent succession planning.

Definition

Innovation-challenge questions are pinpointing exploratory questions formulated to reveal specific organizational or community problems/needs or business opportunities requiring innovative solutions.

In other words, innovation-challenge questions are innovation-related questions or challenges that are strategically formulated, on a continual basis, to reveal a specific need, problem, or opportunity in the context of the organization's value chain or business model to encourage and invoke workforces to generate innovative ideas that specifically target the characteristics of the identified need, problem, or business opportunity.

Importance

Why is it important to understand innovation-challenge questions in relation to innovation talent succession planning?

It is important in that once the functional units have formulated the innovation questions or problems that will be explored in response to various internal and external factors, it is important to know the type of innovation skill sets that the organization will need over a defined period of time to explore the innovation questions or problems that have been identified.

That means that innovation-challenge questions provide data in terms of innovation questions or problems being explored in short and long term by various functional units of the organization. By knowing the type of innovation questions or problems being explored over a certain period, the leadership is able to create an effective innovation talent succession plan that meets the short and long term innovation talent demands based on the innovation questions or problems that functional units have set to explore for innovative solutions.

Chapter Twelve of the *Leadership for Innovation* discusses in detail how to create and manage innovation-challenge questions across functional units.

Step 10: Creating Functional Unit Innovation Goals

Please recall, the main purpose of innovation talent succession planning is to ensure that an organization has adequate talent to meet short and long-term innovation goals and other innovation needs across functional units. We also stated that organizations express innovation goals in different forms such as: achieving short and long-term functional unit and corporate innovation goals. These categories of innovation goals ultimately contribute to realizing the organizational vision. What is the connection between innovation goals and innovation talent succession planning? The connection is that the number of goals will provide data that will help the leadership to determine the type of innovation skill sets that the functional units will need, over a defined period of time based on the various innovation goals across the organization.

This section covers: (1) the definition of innovation goals, (2) why it's important to understand innovation goals in relation to innovation talent succession planning, and (3) how to formulate functional unit innovation goals.

Definition

Innovation goals are statements expressing the desired future state of innovation performance to be attained within a specified period in the context of the specified level of the organization (i.e., individual level, departmental level, corporate level).

Importance

Why is it important to understand functional unit innovation goals in relation to innovation talent succession planning?

Understanding innovation goal setting enables the leadership to determine the type of innovation skills and the number of innovation talent needed by the organization as back-up to achieve short and long-term innovation goals across functional units. This means that each functional unit will be able to understand the extent to which they should deepen and broaden the innovation talent bench-strength to ensure that their functional unit has comfortable levels of innovation skills and competencies required to achieve functional unit goals even if some of the innovation talent have departed.

How to Formulate Functional Unit Innovation Goals

There are a number of aspects to consider when formulating functional unit innovation goals. Chapter Thirteen of *Leadership for Innovation* provides detailed descriptions of aspects to take into consideration when formulating functional unit and corporate goals—and also examples of how to formulate functional unit innovation goals.

Chapter 4

ANALYSIS, INOVATION SKILLS AND RATING

Overview

We have so far looked at Chapters One, Two and Three. Chapter Four covers Steps Eleven, Twelve and Thirteen.

- Step 11: Position Title Analysis in Relation to Innovation Performance
- Step 12: Interpreting Innovation Skills
- Step 13: Creating Rating Scales

Details of the above aspects are as follows:

Step 11: Position Title Analysis in Relation to Innovation Performance

This component involves conducting position title analysis across functional units in order to determine criticality of innovation performance in a job position.

In undertaking this activity, it's important to understand that innovation talent succession planning is a process that should be designed and enacted in all mission-critical positions of the organization. What does this mean? Basically, organization structures are made up of clusters of functional units which are broken down into functional activities aimed at driving the organization mission. Functional activities are structured in job positions, job responsibilities and descriptions, and job specifications. The implementers of functional unit activities are workforces who're endowed with various talents and attributes—and whose individual and team talents provide the force that drive the mission of functional units and the organization as a whole. This section looks at position title analysis in relation to innovation talent succession planning.

The section covers: (1) the definition of position title analysis, (2) why it's important to conduct position title analysis in relation to innovation talent succession planning, and (3) conducting position title analysis.

Definition

This book defines position title analysis as "a process that involves identifying and tabulating various elements of a position title with the view of determining how important the position title is to the innovation performance of the functional unit and the organization as a whole".

Importance

Why is conducting position title analysis important? Two reasons:

Elicitation of data

It is important to understand that like any other skill, innovation skills are expressed in accordance with the innovation performance demands and mandate of a job position. Therefore, position title analysis is important in terms of eliciting data that informs the type of innovation skills, number of innovation talents required to satisfy the "innovation talent bench-strength" level to achieve innovation goals in each functional unit.

Avails information on when innovation skills should be available

Position title analysis provides information on when a particular innovation talent should be available given the prevailing internal and external factors influencing innovation in the functional unit; such information helps the leadership make appropriate decisions on when individuals with the desired level and type of innovation skills (innovation talent bench-strength) should be available in each functional unit.

Conducting Position Title Analysis

For purposes of illustration, we've suggested two tables as example for conducting position title analysis. The tables are separated into two categories: *limited position* and *generic position titles.*

Aspects

Here is a list of some aspects to take into consideration when conducting position title analysis in both limited position and generic position titles:

- Criticality of innovative thinking skills to the position under consideration
- Vulnerability of the position to staff turnover.
- Contribution in terms of innovations (*e.g. product innovation, marketing innovations or other types of innovation)* by the incumbent position holder, at least in the last 5 years
- Evidence of innovation performance by the position holder in the past 5 years
- Criticality of innovation engagement skills and innovation management skills for the position title under consideration
- Innovation engagement and management contribution by the job holder

Let's return to our example of Nada Bank. Assuming Nada Bank provides banking services. There are two activities to be conducted:

First, identify core and support functional units of Nada Bank. Let's assume the Bank has the following functional units:

Core units

- Corporate banking department
- Retail banking department

- E-payments department
- Channel banking department
- Money transfer department
- Marketing department
- Customer service department

Support unit

- HR department
- Finance & accounting department
- IT department
- Corporate affairs department

Second step is to apply tables 3-1 and 3-2 (below) to each of the position titles in all the core and support functional units of Nada Bank.

Table 3-1. Limited Position Titles

Limited Position Titles						
Name of department:			Name of section:			
Position title:						
Criticality of innovative thinking skills	Vulnerability of the position in terms of staff turnover	Contribution in terms of innovation performance by the incumbent position holder in the last 5 years (*e.g. product innovation, service innovation marketing innovation process innovations or other types of innovation)*	Evidence of innovation performance by the position holder in the past 5 years (state number of incremental or radical innovations contributed by the position holder)		Criticality of innovation engagement skills and innovation management skills for this position title	Innovation engagement skills and innovation management skills contribution by the job holder
			Radical innovations	Incremental innovations		
Name of person(s) undertaking the position title analysis:						

Table 3-2. Generic Position Titles

Generic Position Titles						
Name of department:			Name of section:			
Position title:						
Criticality of innovative thinking skills	Vulnerability of the position in terms of staff turnover	Contribution in terms of innovation performance by the incumbent position holder in the last 5 years (e.g. *product innovation, service innovation marketing innovation process innovations, cost-cutting innovations or other types of innovation)*	Evidence or record of innovation performance by the position holder in the past 5 years (state number of incremental or radical innovations contributed by the position holder)		Criticality of innovation engagement skills and innovation management skills for this position title	Innovation engagement skills and innovation management skills contribution by the job holder
			Radical innovations	Incremental innovations		
Name of person(s) undertaking the position title analysis:						

Step 12: Interpreting Innovation Skills

Because of the importance of innovation to growth and competitiveness of organizations, business experts, corporate leaders, and academic researchers have consistently said that innovation is an attainable skill that can be developed, adopted, and applied across industries.

In order to create and sustain practices that drive innovation across functional units, many organizations are making innovation everyone's responsibility across functional units. To realize this, innovation skills are now most sought after across industries.

Step Twelve interprets what innovation skills entail and describes the relationship between innovation skills and innovation talent succession planning. The section covers: (1) the definition of innovation skills, (2) why it's important to understand innovation skills when undertaking innovation talent succession planning, (3) the application of innovation skills, and (4) the interpretation of categories of innovation skills.

Definition

Generally, a skill is defined as the learned ability to carry out a task with pre-determined results. In the context of innovation, this book defines innovation skills as "a combination of abilities that individuals can attain and apply in an organizational context to carry out innovation performance duties and responsibilities and contribute to advancing innovation performance in an organization".

Importance

Why is it important to understand innovation skills in relation to innovation talent succession planning process? Two reasons:

Innovation talent succession planning involves identifying specific innovation skills

Understanding innovation skills is vital because innovation talent succession planning involves identifying and describing specific innovation skill sets required to undertake innovation performance activities across functional units to achieve specific innovation goals. What does this entail? It means that without understanding the different categories or perspectives of innovation skill sets that constitute innovation talent, it will be difficult to identify the right innovation talent required to meet current and future innovation performance needs across functional units, thereby, rendering the innovation talent succession planning ineffective.

Innovation skills are the front and center of innovation talent succession planning

The whole process of innovation succession planning centers on building the required level of "innovation talent bench-strength", consisting of different types and levels of innovation talents across functional units aimed at achieving innovation goals. What this means is that creating an effective innovation talent bench-strength requires the organizational leadership to have an in-depth understanding of different categories of innovation skill sets across functional units and how these skills can be developed. If the leadership has no or little knowledge of innovation skill sets in a broader sense it could lead to creating an innovation talent succession planning that does not focus on real innovation talents needed by functional units.

Application of Innovation Skills

How do you apply innovation skills? Interesting question! In a simple answer, innovation skills can be applied across industries: finance, insurance, health, hospitality, media, entertainment, food, telecommunication, manufacturing and so on. Innovation skills can also be applied by anyone across functional units of organizations in the context of the roles of workforces.

However, innovation performance in organizations does not take place in a vacuum; it is enacted by undertaking innovation-related duties and responsibilities. So, for the workforces to perform innovation roles effectively, it's important for the organizational leadership to understand that innovation roles are separated and performed into three categories: Innovative thinking-related roles, innovation engagement-related roles, and innovation management-related roles. As stated earlier, performing each of the above innovation roles requires skills that relate to each of the innovation-related roles. That being said, the three categories of innovation skills required for executing each of the above innovation-related roles are: innovative thinking skills, innovation engagement skills, and innovation management skills.

Understanding Types of Innovation Skill Sets

Remember, the value of contribution to innovation performance by workforces depends on the level and type of innovation skill set that they possess and how the innovation abilities are applied across functional units. This aspect is critical in innovation talent succession planning, and it is the reason why, as stated earlier, it is important for the organizational leadership to have an in-depth understanding of different categories of innovation skill sets across functional units and how these skills can be developed if an organization is to create an effective innovation talent succession planning.

Here are brief details about each of the three types of innovation skill sets:

- *Innovative thinking skills:* The ability by workforces to identify problems and turn them into innovation opportunities. Chapter One of my book "*Leadership for Innovation*", describes in detail the meaning of innovative thinking skills. Chapter eleven of the "*Leadership for Innovation*", describes in detail the categories of innovation roles and the different types of skill sets.
- *Innovation engagement skills:* Chapter four of the "*Leadership for Innovation*", describes in detail the meaning of innovation engagement skills. Also, chapter eleven of the "*Leadership for Innovation*", describes in detail the categories of innovation roles and the different types of skill sets.
- *Innovation management skills:* Part three of the "*Leadership for Innovation*", describes in detail the meaning of innovation management

skills. Also, chapter eleven of the "*Leadership for Innovation*", describes in detail the categories of innovation roles and the different types of skill sets.

Step 13: Creating Rating Scales

As stated before, the main essence of innovation talent succession planning is to ensure continuity of innovation performance in job positions even after departure of a substantive jobholder. So far, we've covered twelve steps that are necessary for creating and implementing innovation talent succession planning.

Step Thirteen is one of the vital aspects of innovation talent succession planning. In that, the decision by the leadership regarding how much resources should be invested in a job position for innovation talent capacity building initiatives and activities is guided by the data elicited from the rating scales regarding criticality of innovation skills in particular job positions.

The section includes: (1) the purpose of rating scales, (2) the importance of the rating scales in relation to innovation talent succession planning, and (3) examples of categories of innovation skills in a job position, innovation abilities of jobholders, and talent turnover vulnerability rating scales.

Purpose

The purpose of the rating scales is to elicit data about three aspects:

- Criticality of innovation skills in a position
- Innovation abilities of jobholder
- Innovation talent turnover vulnerability of a position

This information is then applied in the decision-making process regarding the type and level of innovation skill sets and competencies required in a job for both short and long-term to realize the innovation objectives of the functional unit.

Importance

Why is it important to determine innovation skills in job positions, innovation abilities of jobholder, and talent turnover vulnerability of job positions when undertaking innovation talent succession planning?

In order to create innovation talent succession planning with an effective innovation talent bench-strength that meets short and long term needs of the organization, it's vital that the organizational leadership elicits (by use of the rating scales) accurate information about the three vital aspects.

The information derived from the rating scales aligned to each of the above three aspects is applied to make decisions about the type and level of innovation skill sets, and number of innovation talent required in each job position.

To put it differently, it is very difficult to accurately make decisions about innovation talent bench-strength across functional units without information about the three aspects; namely, criticality of innovation skills in each position, innovation abilities of the job holder, and innovation talent turnover rate in job positions, thus, the necessity and importance of the rating of the aforementioned aspects.

Examples of Rating Scales

Here are examples of the categories of rating scales for determining the three aspects:

- Criticality of the three innovation skills in a job position
- Innovation abilities of incumbent job holder
- Innovation talent turnover vulnerability of the position

Determining criticality of the three innovation skills in a job position i.e.

- Scale I: Innovative thinking skills
- Scale II: Innovation engagement skills
- Scale III: Innovation management skills

Scale I

Criticality of innovative thinking skills	Not critical	Slightly Critical	Moderately Critical	Very Critical	Extremely Critical
	1	2	3	4	5

Scale II

Criticality of innovation engagement skills	Not critical	Slightly Critical	Moderately Critical	Very Critical	Extremely Critical
	1	2	3	4	5

Scale III

Criticality of innovation management skills	Not critical	Slightly Critical	Moderately Critical	Very Critical	Extremely Critical
	1	2	3	4	5

Innovation abilities of incumbent position holder, in terms of:

- Scale I: Generation of innovative ideas in the context of the functional unit activities
- Scale II: Development and implementation of innovation engagement-related initiatives and programs
- Scale III: Development and implementation of innovation management-related strategies and initiatives

Scale III

Innovation performance of jobholder in terms of generation of innovative ideas in the last five years in the context of the activities of the functional unit	Not good	Fair	Good	Very good	Excellent
	1	2	3	4	5

Scale II

Innovation engagement-related initiatives developed or contributed by the jobholder	Poor	Fair	Good	Very good	Excellent
	1	2	3	4	5

Scale III

Innovation management-related-initiatives developed or contributed by the jobholder	Poor	Fair	Good	Very good	Excellent
	1	2	3	4	5

Determine innovation talent turnover vulnerability of job position

Vulnerability could be determined by the number of innovation talent departures that a position under consideration experiences over a specified period of time—could be two to five years. Based on the number of departures, the simple scale below could be used to determine or predict vulnerability of a job position.

Innovation talent turnover vulnerability of the job position	Not vulnerable	Slightly vulnerable	Moderately vulnerable	Very vulnerable	Extremely vulnerable
	1	2	3	4	5

Chapter 5

METRICS AND IMPLEMENTATION PLANS

Overview

Remember, we have so far looked at thirteen steps segmented into four chapters of creating a framework for innovation talent succession planning. Chapter Five looks at the last steps:

- Step 14: Metrics for Determining Innovation Abilities of Position Holder
- Step 15: Developing and Implementing Innovation Skill Bench-Strength Plans

Step 14: Metrics for Determining Innovation Abilities of Position Holder

This section prescribes how to determine innovation skills and abilities in position holders when conducting innovation talent succession planning.

As stated before, the essence of this book is to suggest tools to help organizations build sufficient innovation talent bench-strength across functional units so that achievement of functional unit and corporate innovation goals is not affected when employees with specific innovation skills depart the position or the organization.

In the thirteen steps covered so far, we've suggested some tools that are necessary and essential when conducting innovation talent succession planning. Step Fourteen is one of the vital elements of the innovation talent succession planning. The section covers: (1) why it's important to determine innovation abilities in position holders and (2) how to determine innovation abilities and competencies in position holders.

Importance

Why is it important to determine innovation abilities in position holders when conducting innovation talent succession planning? Two reasons:

Provides insight of innovation abilities and competencies across functional units

Remember, the ultimate purpose of innovation talent succession planning is to provide insurance of the innovation performance capability to functional units when they (the functional units) experience innovation talent departures.

The insurance of innovation performance continuity would only be secured if the leadership had insight of the innovation abilities and competencies of all position holders across functional units. Therefore, it is vital for the leadership to have insight of how the innovation skill sets and abilities are spread across position holders in each functional unit.

Helps to identify areas of innovation skill strengths and weaknesses in each incumbent position holder

Thus far, we know that there are three categories of innovation skills namely, innovative thinking skills, innovation engagement skills and innovation management skills. In relation to these categories of innovation skill sets, the leadership should ensure that all functional units have, at all times, an innovation talent bench-strength that comprises teams with a mix of all the needed mission-critical innovation abilities, and the leadership should also be able to identify areas of innovation skill strengths and weaknesses in each incumbent position holder. However, identifying areas of strength and weaknesses in innovation abilities of position holders would only be possible if the organization has tools for eliciting information about all the three categories of innovation skill sets and abilities in incumbent position holders.

Determining Innovation Abilities in Position Holders

The second aspect is determining innovation abilities of position holders across functional units. *How do you do that?* This section has suggested some techniques for determining the level of all the three types or categories of innovation skills and abilities; that is, *innovative thinking skills, innovation engagement skills,* and *innovation management skills* in position holders. We illustrate how each of the three types innovation abilities can be determined as follows:

Innovative Thinking Skills

There are six aspects that could be used to determine innovative thinking skills and abilities in position holders. Each aspect is outlined in the six tables designed to elicit specific information in relation to the aspect under consideration. There are six tables labelled: 3-3, 3-4, 3-5, 3-6, 3-7, 3-8. Each table focuses on the aspect under consideration.

- Description of innovation patents generated by the position holder (Table 3-3).
- Description of team-generated innovation patents in which the position holder was involved (Table 3-4)
- Description of unpatented (launched) innovations generated by the position holder (Table 3-5)
- Description of unpatented (launched) team-generated innovations in which the position holder was involved (Table 3-6)
- Description of innovation ideas generated by the position holder and undergoing development (Table 3-7)
- Description of team-generated innovation ideas that are undergoing development in which the position holder was involved (Table 3-8)

Table 3-3. Innovation Patents Generated by the Position Holder

Position title:	Name of position holder:
Indicate whether the position is *limited* or *generic:*	
Description of innovation patents generated by the position holder	
1	
2	
3	
4	
5	
Name of staff responsible compiling the information:	
Date when information was collected:	

Table 3-4. Team-Generated Innovation Patents in which the Position Holder was Involved

Position title:	Name of position holder:
Description of team-generated innovation patents in which the position holder had participated	
1	
2	
3	
4	
5	
Name of staff responsible compiling the information:	
Date when information was collected:	

Table 3-5. Unpatented (Launched) Innovations *(Revenue and Cost Saving Innovations)* Generated by the Position Holder

Position title: Name of position holder:	
Description of unpatented (*launched*) innovations generated by the position holder:	
List revenue-generating innovations by the position holder:	List cost-saving innovations generated by the position holder unit:
Name of staff responsible compiling the information:	
Date when information was collected:	

Table 3-6. Unpatented (Launched) Team-Generated Innovations (*Revenue and Cost-Saving Innovations*) in which the Position Holder was Involved

Position title: Name of position holder:	
Description of unpatented (*launched*) team-generated innovations in which the position holder was involved:	
List revenue-generating innovations in which the position holder was involved:	List cost-saving innovations generated in which the position holder was involved:
Name of staff responsible compiling the information:	
Date when information was collected:	

Table 3-7. Innovative Ideas (*Revenue and Cost Saving*) Undergoing Development Generated by the Position Holder

Position title: Name of position holder:	
Description of innovative ideas (*revenue and cost saving*) undergoing development generated by the position holder:	
List revenue-generating innovations in which the position holder was involved:	List cost-saving innovations generated in which the position holder was involved:
Name of staff responsible compiling the information:	
Date when information was collected:	

Table 3-8. Team-Generated Innovative Ideas (*Revenue and Cost Saving*) Undergoing Development in which the Position Holder Was Involved

Position title: Name of position holder:	
Description of team-generated innovative ideas (*revenue and cost saving*) undergoing development in which the position holder was involved:	
List revenue-generating innovations in which the position holder was involved:	List cost-saving innovations generated in which the position holder was involved:
Name of staff responsible compiling the information:	
Date when information was collected:	

Innovation Engagement Skills

Remember, in Step Twelve, when discussing the aspect of interpreting the three types of innovation skills—namely, innovative thinking skills, innovation engagement skills, and innovation management skills, we advised to refer to Chapters One and Four of my previous book, "*Leadership for Innovation*", for details about the meaning of innovative thinking skills and innovation engagement skills, respectively. In a nutshell, innovation engagement skills are the ability to develop and implement, on a regular basis, a variety of initiatives aimed at instilling innovation in the hearts and minds of workforces across functional units.

Below is an example of a table for determining innovation engagement skills in position holders.

Table 3-9. Determining Innovation Engagement Skills in Position Holders

Position title:	Name of position holder:
Description of the innovation engagement-related programs initiated by the position holder:	
1	
2	
3	
4	
5	
Name of staff responsible compiling the information:	
Date when information was collected:	

Innovation Management Skills

On the other hand, as stated before, *innovation management skills* are the abilities that enable position holders to formulate and implement innovation-support strategies, policies, and procedures on a regular basis, aimed at building climate for innovation across functional units. Below is an example of a table for determining innovation management skills in position holders.

Table 3-10. Determining Innovation Management Skills in Position Holders

Position title:	Name of position holder:
Description of the innovation management-related strategies, policies and procedures initiated by the position holder:	
1	
2	
3	
4	
5	
Name of staff responsible compiling the information:	
Date when information was collected:	

Step 15: Developing and Implementing Innovation Skill Bench-Strength Plans

So far we understand that the main purpose of innovation talent succession planning is twofold: (1) to regularly assess innovation skill bench-strength across functional units of the organizations (2) then make decisions about approaches and programs that the leadership needs to implement to ensure that the organization has a deep innovation skill bench-strength in tandem with the short and long term innovation goals of the functional units across the organization.

We defined innovation talent succession planning as: a process that involves making decisions and taking actions to create a pool of innovation talent with the right mix of innovation skill sets so that the innovation performance of functional units is not adversely affected in case of innovation talent movements, as functional units will have talent to potentially succeed incumbent position holders and successfully perform innovation functions.

The implication of the above definition is that the process of innovation talent succession planning is centered on the planning and execution of specific innovation talent succession-related activities so that continuity of innovation performance is maintained in case of innovation talent movements. At the fulcrum of innovation talent succession-related activities is the innovation skill bench-strength plan, also referred to as "innovation talent succession plan".

The innovation skill bench-strength plan is an outline of various activities intended to create the required level of innovation skills bench-strength in all mission-critical job positions across functional units of an organization. This is the focus of Step Fifteen. The section looks at: (1) the definition of innovation skills bench-strength plan, (2) the importance of innovation skills bench-strength plans, (3) an example of how to develop and execute an innovation skills bench-strength plan, and (4) where the responsibility lies for creating the innovation skills bench-strength plan.

Definition

The innovation skills bench-strength plan is: *A set of guidelines and steps on how to manage activities aimed at building a pool of innovation talent bench-strength across functional units on a daily, weekly, monthly, and yearly basis.*

Importance

It's vital to understand that the process of innovation talent succession planning does not take place in a vacuum, it involves a series planning and execution of related actions and activities aimed at achieving the goal of building a sufficient pool of innovation talent across functional units. Building a pool of innovation talent depends on how well the innovation skills bench-strength plan is formulated. There are two reasons why an innovation skills bench-strength plan is important:

Data is tabulated and analysed at this stage

The first reason why an innovation skills bench-strength plan is important is this is the stage where data about innovation skill requirements and availability in each job position is tabulated and analysed. Such data includes:

- Criticality of innovation skills in a job position
- Expected level of innovation competencies in a job position
- Information about the retirement status of jobholder
- Vulnerability of position to staff turnover
- Current innovation skills bench-strength of a job position
- Innovation performance abilities of the current job holder
- Innovation skills development objectives
- Innovation skills bench-strength development plan
- Innovation skills development interventions

Provides guidelines on how to manage innovation skills bench-strength activities

Tabulation and analysis of data do not mean anything if the data is not applied to realize the intended purpose. So, the second reason an innovation skills bench-strength plan is important is that it provides guidelines on how each functional unit will manage activities relating to building a pool of innovation skills bench-strength on a daily, weekly, monthly, and yearly basis.

Responsibility for Creating Innovation Skills Bench-Strength Plan

Who should be responsible for creating the innovation skills bench-strength plan? Since innovation talent succession planning is a human capital component, the development and implementation of the innovation skills bench-strength plan should be the responsibility of Human Resources. In the absence of a stand-alone HR functional unit, the innovation skills bench-strength plan can be delegated to either a committee or a functional unit that management sees fit to undertake the process. Either way, it's important for the team undertaking the innovation skills bench-strength plan to confer and collaborate with the heads of all functional units across the organization for their input in creating the plan.

Example: Developing an Innovation Skills Bench-Strength Plan

How would you create an innovation talent succession plan (also referred to as innovation skills bench-strength plan)? Let's return to our example of Nada Bank. First, identify core and support functional units of Nada Bank, as follows:

Core Units

- Corporate banking department
- Retail banking department
- E-payments department
- Channel banking department
- Money transfer department
- Marketing department
- Customer service department

Support Unit

- HR department
- Finance and accounting department
- IT department
- Corporate affairs department

Second, is to understand that developing an innovation talent succession plan (or the innovation skills bench-strength plan) for job positions in the above functional units would involve taking the following considerations:

- Identify mission-critical positions in both core and support functional units.
- Determine the number of limited position titles and generic position titles in both core and support functional units.
- Create tables for tabulating and analysing data relating to different aspects of the innovation talent succession plan.

Tables

We have suggested tables to demonstrate how pertinent aspects can be tabulated and analysed into meaningful data for creating the innovation skills bench-strength plan. Examples of the tables:

- Table 3-11: Position analysis
- Table 3-12: Description of innovation performance abilities
- Table 3-13: Innovation skills development objectives
- Table 3-14: Innovation skill bench-strength development plan
- Table 3-15: Innovation skills development interventions

Outlined as follows:

- **Table 3-11:** Position analysis, includes the following aspects:
    - Vulnerability of position to workforce turnover
    - Retirement status of the incumbent position holder
    - Criticality of each of the three types or categories of innovation skill sets: *innovative thinking, innovation engagement, and innovation management* to the position under consideration
    - Competency rating of the incumbent position holder in the last 5 years in each of the innovation skills: *innovative thinking, innovation engagement, and innovation management*

- Acceptable level of rating performance for each of the innovation skills: *innovative thinking, innovation leadership, and innovation management* for the position under consideration
- Innovative thinking performance of the incumbent position holder in the last 5 years

The above aspects would be stated in the table below:

Table 3-11. Position Analysis

<table>
<tr><td colspan="4">Department:

Position title: Name of position holder:

State whether the position is limited or generic:

Date:</td></tr>
<tr><td colspan="4">Position analysis and rating comments</td></tr>
<tr><td>Aspects for position analysis</td><td colspan="3">Rating comments</td></tr>
<tr><td>1. Vulnerability of position to workforce turnover</td><td>Green</td><td>Yellow</td><td>Red</td></tr>
<tr><td colspan="4">Interpretation of the colors:
• Green denotes low vulnerability
• Yellow denotes highly vulnerable
• Red denotes extremely vulnerable</td></tr>
<tr><td>2. Retirement status of the incumbent position holder</td><td>Green</td><td>Yellow</td><td>Red</td></tr>
<tr><td colspan="4">Interpretation of the colors:
• Green denotes not close to retiring
• Yellow nearing retirement
• Red due for retirement</td></tr>
</table>

table continues on next page

<table>
<tr><td rowspan="2">3. Criticality of each of the three types or categories of innovation skill sets: innovative thinking, innovation engagement and innovation management to the position under consideration</td><td>Innovative thinking abilities</td><td>Innovation engagement abilities</td><td>Innovation Management abilities</td></tr>
<tr><td></td><td></td><td></td></tr>
<tr><td colspan="4">Note: Use the rating scale below to determine and to state criticality of each of the above three types or categories of innovation abilities
<table>
<tr><td>Not Critical</td><td>Slightly Critical</td><td>Moderately Critical</td><td>Very Critical</td><td>Extremely Critical</td></tr>
<tr><td>1</td><td>2</td><td>3</td><td>4</td><td>5</td></tr>
</table></td></tr>
<tr><td rowspan="2">4. Competency rating of the incumbent position holder in the last 5 years in each of the innovation skills: innovative thinking, innovation engagement and innovation management</td><td>Innovative thinking abilities</td><td>Innovation engagement abilities</td><td>Innovation management abilities</td></tr>
<tr><td></td><td></td><td></td></tr>
<tr><td colspan="4">Note: Use the scale below to rate of each of the above three categories or types of innovation abilities
<table>
<tr><td>Poor</td><td>Fair</td><td>Good</td><td>Very good</td><td>Excellent</td></tr>
<tr><td>1</td><td>2</td><td>3</td><td>4</td><td>5</td></tr>
</table></td></tr>
</table>

table continues on next page

	Innovative thinking	Innovation engagement	Innovation management
5. Acceptable level of rating performance of each of the innovation skills: *innovative thinking, innovation leadership, and innovation management* for the position under consideration			

Note: *Use the scale below to rate of each of the above three categories or types of innovation abilities for the position under consideration*

Poor	Fair	Good	Very good	Excellent
1	2	3	4	5

6. Innovative thinking performance of the incumbent position holder in the last 5 years

Innovative thinking rating scale

Poor	Fair	Good	Very good	Excellent
1	2	3	4	5

Table 3-12: Outline of Innovation Skills Bench-Strength and Gaps

Current Innovation Skills Bench-Strength and Gaps in the Position Under Consideration						
Department: Name and position of staff outlining the strength and gaps: Date:						
Position of under consider-ation:	Innovative thinking abilities		Innovation engagement abilities		Innovation management abilities	
	Strengths	Gaps	Strengths	Gaps	Strengths	Gaps
1.						
2.						
3.						
4.						
5.						
	How do you rate the overall bench-strength of innovative thinking competencies in the position under consideration?		How do you rate the overall bench-strength of innovation engagement competencies in the position under consideration?		How do you rate the overall bench-strength of innovation management competencies in the position under consideration?	

table continues on next page

Below is an example of rating scale that can be used to determine the three perspectives of the innovation performance above:

Very low	Low	Adequate	High	Very high
1	2	3	4	5

Table 3-13: Innovation Skills Development Objectives

Department:

Name and position of staff outlining the objectives:

Date:

Innovation skills development objectives

To ensure that the functional unit "W" has "X" number of staff in "Y" months who are able to perform the following categories of innovation roles:

Innovative thinking roles	**Innovation engagement roles**	**Innovation management roles**
Translate the innovative thinking roles in the context of the functional unit under consideration	Translate the innovation engagement roles in the context of the functional unit under consideration	Translate the innovation management roles in the context of the functional unit under consideration

Table 3-14: Innovation Skill Bench-Strength Development Plan

The following are some of the aspects that would be included when creating an innovation skill bench-strength development plan.

- Workforce innovation development initiatives to be undertaken.
- Timeframe within which implementation of the workforce development initiatives would be undertaken.
- Names of staff involved in co-ordinating the workforce development initiatives and programs.
- Resources needed for the workforce innovation development initiatives and activities.
- Timeframe within which the innovation skill bench-strength plan will be developed.
- Expected outcomes in terms of the number of workforces and type of innovation skills needed to create the required innovation talent bench-strength.
- Frequent evaluations to determine how each functional unit was progressing toward its goal of attaining the required level of the innovation skill bench- strength.

Below is an example of a table for creating an innovation skill bench-strength development plan.

Table 3-14. Innovation Skill Bench-Strength Development Plan

<table>
<tr><td colspan="6">Name of functional unit:

Number of position titles:

Number of limited position titles:

Number of generic position titles:</td></tr>
<tr><td>Workforce innovation devel-opment initiatives to be un-dertaken</td><td>Timeframe for imple-mentation of the workforce innovation devel-opment initiatives</td><td>Staff involved in coordi-nating de-velopment programs</td><td>Resources needed for devel-opment programs</td><td>Timeframe within which innova-tion talent bench-strength plan would be devel-oped</td><td>Expected outcomes in terms of number workforces and type of innova-tion skills earmarked to be de-veloped</td></tr>
<tr><td></td><td></td><td></td><td></td><td></td><td></td></tr>
<tr><td></td><td></td><td></td><td></td><td></td><td></td></tr>
<tr><td></td><td></td><td></td><td></td><td></td><td></td></tr>
<tr><td colspan="6">Evaluations: Regular evaluations should be conducted to determine how each functional unit was progressing toward its goal of attaining the required number and type of innovation skills bench- strength required</td></tr>
<tr><td>Date:</td><td>Date:</td><td>Date:</td><td>Date:</td><td>Date:</td><td>Date:</td></tr>
<tr><td>Outline the aspects that will be evaluated on this date</td><td>Outline the aspects that will be evaluated on this date</td><td>Outline the aspects that will be evaluated on this date</td><td>Outline the aspects that will be evaluated on this date</td><td>Outline the aspects that will be evaluated on this date</td><td>Outline the aspects that will be evaluated on this date</td></tr>
</table>

Table 3-15: Innovation Skills Development Interventions

<table>
<tr><td colspan="3">Developing interventions to deal with the innovation skills-gaps in the functional units earmarked for innovation skill bench-strength</td></tr>
<tr><td colspan="3">Name of functional unit:

Number of position titles:

Number of limited position titles:

Number of generic position titles:</td></tr>
<tr><th>Interventions for gaps in innovative thinking abilities</th><th>Interventions for gaps in innovation engagement abilities</th><th>Interventions for gaps in innovation management abilities</th></tr>
<tr><td>• Appropriate training approaches aimed at enhancing innovative thinking abilities and attributes.
• Other interventions could include mentoring, coaching, kind of internships or attachments to highly innovative companies, etc.</td><td>• Appropriate training approaches aimed at enhancing innovation engagement abilities
• Other interventions could include mentoring, coaching, kind of internships or attachments to companies with a strong innovation culture</td><td>• Appropriate training approaches aimed at enhancing innovation management abilities
• Other interventions could include mentoring, coaching, kind of internships or attachments to companies with a strong innovation culture</td></tr>
</table>

Aspects to consider

Here are some aspects to take into consideration when creating innovation skill bench-strength plans:

- The head of the human resources unit or learning and development manager should regularly confer and collaborate with the heads of the respective departments to produce staff development plans and programs on the three types of innovation skills, i.e. innovative thinking skills, innovation engagement skills, and innovation management skills.

- Look out for other non-innovation abilities (the technical competencies) that staff could be lacking because enhancement of technical competencies of staff also contributes to strengthening their innovation performance abilities of staff.
- Staff development plans should take into consideration two aspects: (1) the vulnerability of position to staff turnover and (2) the retirement status of staff across functional units. If the rating on the vulnerability scale indicates that the position is vulnerable to workforce turnover and the retirement scale shows the incumbent position holders are nearing retirement, it means that you should quicken your plans for building the required level of the innovation skill bench-strength.

SUMMARY

Let's recap the four main aspects the book has covered:

1. Without the appropriate tools, it is difficult to effectively determine the following in an organization:
   - Present innovation performance needs
   - Present innovation skill set needs
   - Future innovation performance needs
   - Future innovation skill set needs
2. Understanding current and future innovation skill set needs analytics of the organization is a critical aspect of creating and sustaining a culture of innovation in organizations.
3. Structured in fifteen steps, the book is segmented in five chapters for designing and implementing a framework for creating an innovation talent succession plan in organizations.
4. Prescribes tools for creating a pool of workforces with right mix of innovation skill sets so that innovation performance of functional units or achievement of short or long-term innovation goals is not negatively affected in case of innovation talent departures.

SELECTED REFERENCES

https://www.forbes.com/sites/timworstall/2015/02/09/elon-musk-has-raided-150-people-from-apple-for-tesla/#726883544b80

https://www.cipd.co.uk/Images/resourcing-talent-planning_2015_tcm18-11303.pdf

https://www.prnewswire.com/news-releases/manpowergroup-annual-survey-reveals-one-third-of-employers-worldwide-cannot-find-qualified-talent-despite-over-supply-of-available-workers-122210438.html

https://home.kpmg/content/dam/kpmg/pdf/2014/07/war-for-talent.pdf

https://www.bcg.com/publications/2015/growth-lean-manufacturing-innovation-in-2015.aspx

https://www.pwc.com/gx/en/ceo-survey/2017/deep-dives/ceo-survey-global-talent.pdf

David Masumba, *Leadership for Innovation: Three Essential Skills for Leading Employee Driven Innovation,* Morgan James, 2019.

www.ingramcontent.com/pod-product-compliance
Lightning Source LLC
LaVergne TN
LVHW051019080826
845145LV00009B/2702

* 9 7 8 1 7 3 4 1 9 1 3 5 6 *